Dear Parents and Educators,

Welcome to Penguin Young Readers! As parents and educators, you know that each child develops at his or her own pace—in terms of speech, critical thinking, and, of course, reading. Penguin Young Readers recognizes this fact. As a result, each Penguin Young Readers book is assigned a traditional easy-to-read level (1–4) as well as a Guided Reading Level (A–P). Both of these systems will help you choose the right book for your child. Please refer to the back of each book for specific leveling information. Penguin Young Readers features esteemed authors and illustrators, stories about favorite characters, fascinating nonfiction, and more!

Egyptian Gods and Goddesses

LEVEL 4

GUIDED READING LEVEL N

This book is perfect for a **Fluent Reader** who:
- can read the text quickly with minimal effort;
- has good comprehension skills;
- can self-correct (can recognize when something doesn't sound right); and
- can read aloud smoothly and with expression.

Here are some **activities** you can do during and after reading this book:
- Comprehension: Answer the following questions.
  - How did the dead person get to the Underworld safely?
  - What were some of the dangers on the way to the Underworld?
  - What did it mean when a person's heart weighed the same as the Feather of Truth?
  - What happened when a person's heart weighed more than the Feather of Truth?
  - What was inside some of the Egyptians' tombs?
- Research: Do your own research on one of the gods you read about in the book—Horus, Re, Thoth, Montu, Osiris, Isis. What other facts can you find out?

Remember, sharing the love of reading with a child is the best gift you can give!

—Bonnie Bader, EdM
   Penguin Young Readers program

*Penguin Young Readers are leveled by independent reviewers applying the standards developed by Irene Fountas and Gay Su Pinnell in *Matching Books to Readers: Using Leveled Books in Guided Reading*, Heinemann, 1999.

Penguin Young Readers
Published by the Penguin Group
Penguin Group (USA) Inc., 375 Hudson Street, New York, New York 10014, USA
Penguin Group (Canada), 90 Eglinton Avenue East, Suite 700, Toronto, Ontario M4P 2Y3, Canada
(a division of Pearson Penguin Canada Inc.)
Penguin Books Ltd., 80 Strand, London WC2R 0RL, England
Penguin Group Ireland, 25 St. Stephen's Green, Dublin 2, Ireland (a division of Penguin Books Ltd.)
Penguin Group (Australia), 250 Camberwell Road, Camberwell, Victoria 3124, Australia
(a division of Pearson Australia Group Pty. Ltd.)
Penguin Books India Pvt. Ltd., 11 Community Centre, Panchsheel Park, New Delhi—110 017, India
Penguin Group (NZ), 67 Apollo Drive, Rosedale, Auckland 0632, New Zealand
(a division of Pearson New Zealand Ltd.)
Penguin Books (South Africa) (Pty.) Ltd., 24 Sturdee Avenue,
Rosebank, Johannesburg 2196, South Africa

Penguin Books Ltd., Registered Offices: 80 Strand, London WC2R 0RL, England

Text copyright © 1999 by Henry Barker. Cover illustration copyright © 1999 by Jenny Williams.
Interior illustrations copyright © 1999 by Jeff Crosby. All rights reserved. First published in 1999 by
Grosset & Dunlap, an imprint of Penguin Group (USA) Inc. Published in 2012 by Penguin Young
Readers, an imprint of Penguin Group (USA) Inc., 345 Hudson Street, New York, New York 10014.
Manufactured in China.

Library of Congress Control Number: 99026971

ISBN 978-0-448-42029-5   10 9 8 7 6 5 4 3 2 1

PENGUIN YOUNG READERS

LEVEL
FLUENT READER
4

EGYPTIAN
Gods and Goddesses

by Henry Barker
illustrated by Jeff Crosby
cover illustrated by Jenny Williams

Penguin Young Readers
An Imprint of Penguin Group (USA) Inc.

It is more than 3,000 years ago in Egypt. There is a festival in honor of Horus.

Horus was the king of the gods.

The people of ancient Egypt prayed to many gods. There were more than 1,000.

Some looked like animals.

Some looked like people.

Some had the head of an animal and
the body of a person.

Each one had special powers.

Re brought the warmth of the sun.

Because of Thoth, there was the light of the moon.

Montu guarded warriors in battle.

All these gods protected life on earth.

Other gods ruled the Land of the Dead—Osiris, Isis, and Anubis.

They were very powerful.

The Egyptians believed that
after a person died, his soul went
to the Underworld.

There were many dangers on the way.

There were snakes. There were lakes of fire. There were demons.

So there were special rules to travel there safely.

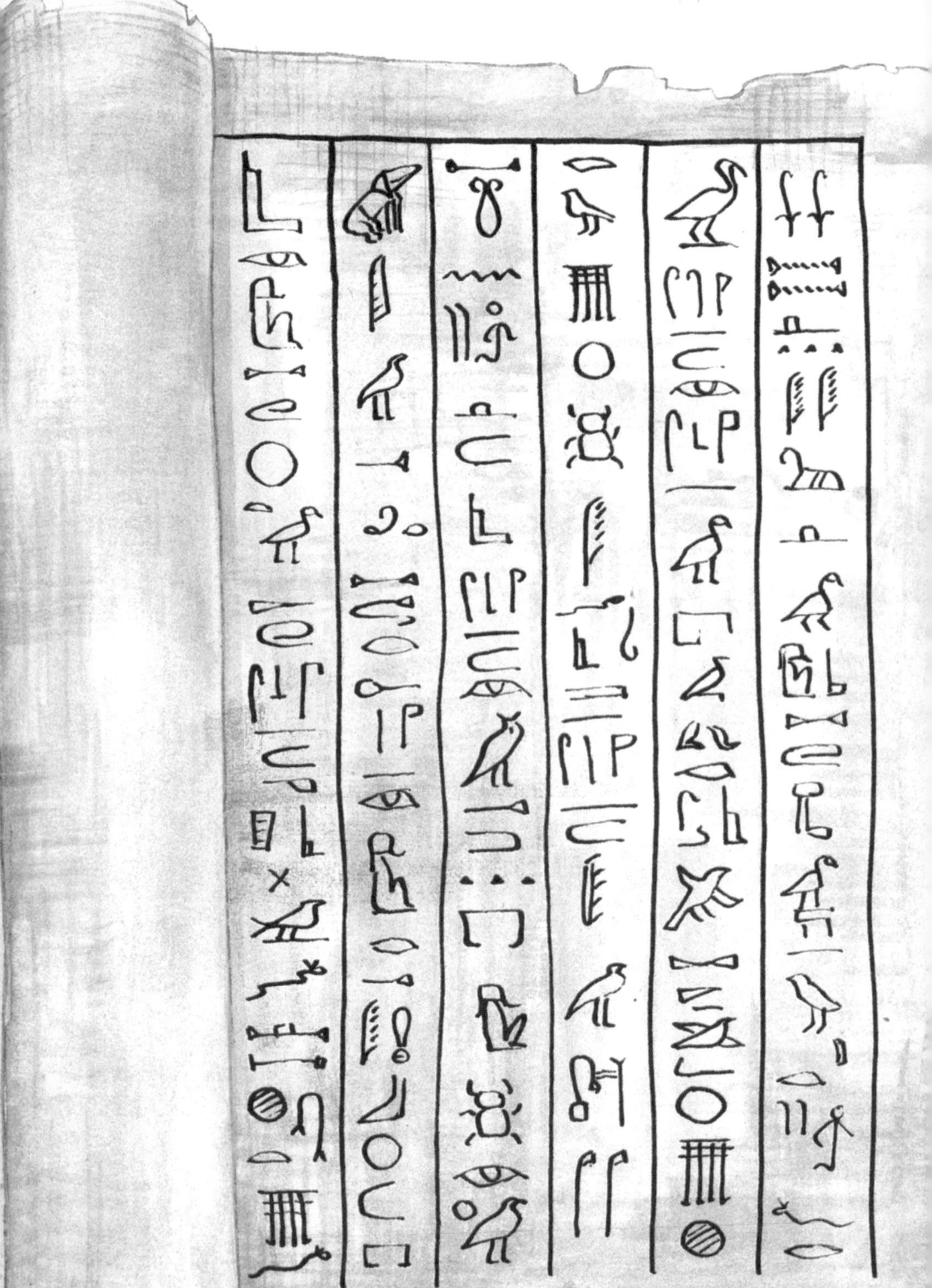

The dead person used magic spells,
prayers, and maps. The spells came from
"The Book of the Dead." They helped
the person get to the Hall of Judgment.

There, Osiris, the ruler of the
Underworld, greeted the dead person.

The person had to swear that his life had been good.

Osiris asked many questions.

If the person's answers pleased the gods, then came the most important test.

It was the Weighing of the Heart.
Anubis held up a scale.

A goddess named Maat placed her
Feather of Truth on one side of the scale.

She placed the dead person's heart
on the other side.

The gods watched carefully.

A monster with the head of a crocodile sat close to the scale.

Did the feather and the heart weigh the same? If they did, it meant the dead person had been good.

So the person would go to a beautiful place—the Field of Reeds. And like a god, he would live forever.

But what if the heart was heavier than the feather?

That meant the dead person had been bad.

Then the crocodile monster would eat
the heart with her sharp teeth!
No one wanted that to happen.

All Egyptians wanted to enjoy a wonderful afterlife. And it took more than being good.

30

The soul needed a body to come
"home" to. So they learned how to keep
a dead body from rotting away.

They learned how to make mummies.

Making a mummy took a long time.
Priests in special masks helped with
the work.

First the organs were taken out of
the body.

Then the body was put in special salt.
The salt dried out the body. This took
40 days. After that came a coating of oil
and wax.

Finally, the body was stuffed with cloth or sand and wrapped in linen strips. The organs were put in special jars.

The ancient Egyptians became very good at making mummies.

Some have lasted for thousands of years.

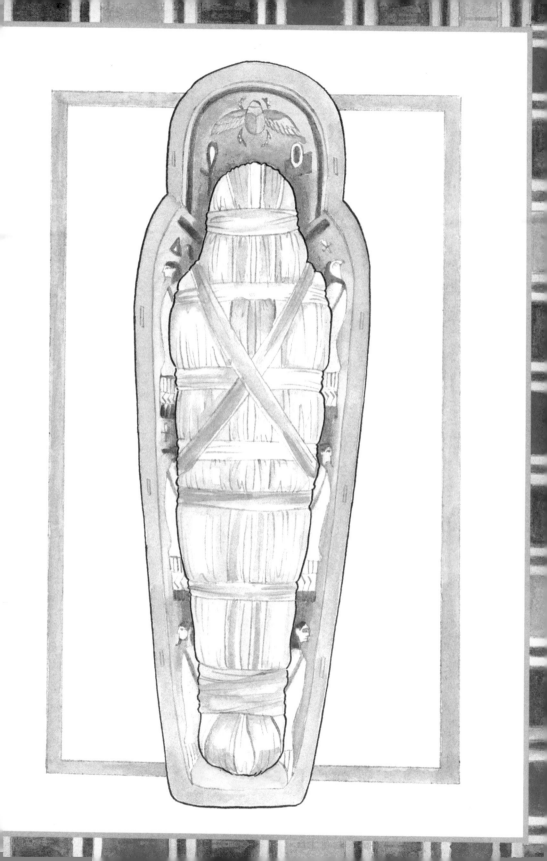

The Egyptians also thought that
mummies had to have special houses. So
they built tombs for them.

They built all kinds.

Some were small—just holes in the
ground.

Others were huge.

Three of the biggest tombs are still standing. They are called the Great Pyramids.

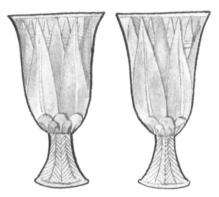

Rich Egyptians wanted to enjoy their afterlife. They wanted it to be like their lives on earth. So they had their tombs filled with food, jewelry, furniture, games, and musical instruments.

Statues of workers and servants went into the tombs, too.

The Egyptians believed that the statues would come to life and work for the dead person.

Some tombs even had animal mummies.

They had been the pets of the
dead person.

Do people in Egypt still believe in the old gods?

Do they still make mummies?

No. Their religion changed long, long ago.

Today most Egyptians are Muslims.

They no longer pray to Horus or Osiris or Isis.

They pray to one god—Allah.

But every year thousands of people visit the ancient temples. There they see the old gods, frozen in time.

Have the old gods lost their power?
Perhaps. But they will never be forgotten.